CONTENTS

Introduction	3
Chapter 1	4
Our Great Canal Journey	5
Chapter 2	7
The Purchase	8
Chapter 3	25
Applying to be on Amazing Spaces	26
Chapter 4	36
The Rear Cut	37
Chapter 5	44
The Build	45
Chapter 6	69
The Front Cut	70
Chapter 7	79
The Reveal	80

1

Jayne Walden

Matilda Jayne
Our Great Canal Journey

BY
Jayne Walden

DEDICATION

Thank you to George and all the team at Amazing Spaces for making it happen and trusting in Billy to pull off such a big build.

Thank you to all my friends and family that have supported Billy in his journey, particularly Matilda who put up with all the stress and her bedtime stories being rushed.

Thank you to Aunty Issy Carr and Billy's fourth emergency service Wee Bill.

CHAPTER 1

◆ ◆ ◆

OUR GREAT CANAL JOURNEY

❖ ❖ ❖

Billy, Matilda and I were all in the cab of our much-loved truck, a Volkswagen LT, Vera. We were driving along in silence and apart from concentrating on the road ahead, I was not thinking of very much, mundane thoughts were just floating around in my head; like the first fall of delicate snowflakes, fluttering and dancing in the night sky, struggling to the ground and attach themselves to something secure. Suddenly the silence was broken with an abrupt yell, out of the blue my son, Billy blurted out", Why don't we get a canal boat?"

Billy then put up a damn good argument, which wouldn't have looked that out of place if it was coming out of the mouth of an accomplished QC. Billy didn't stop there, he carried on explaining that we could buy a narrowboat, maybe one which was totally dilapidated and refurbish it, he then added that it could be a wonderful family project and how when it was completed, we could all go off cruising the waterways exploring England at a leisurely 4 miles an hour.

Whilst Billy had been wittering on stating his case, I had pulled Vera up in a layby, I was now sitting sideways in the cab staring at him in disbelief. Where I'd parked the wagon, just happened to be next to the canal, the beauty of this spot helped to cement Billy's argument. Matilda was already siding with Billy and needed little encouragement to throw herself head first into our new adventure. They both tried to convince me that this was the best idea since sliced bread and why in my 40 years on this earth, I had not had the good sense to think of it previously. Matilda looked at me with that look, reminiscent of an old school teacher looking over his bi focal glasses when you had been naughty, her look screamed 'honestly mother, you know why you've never thought of this before.'

Well, there are two main answers to that and a couple of obvious flaws in Billy's cunning plan, one was 'the joining together as a family to refurbish it', I hardly knew one end of the hammer from another and the other and most important, was we were skint.

CHAPTER 2

THE PURCHASE

◆ ◆ ◆

So that is how we came to buy MatildaJayne. I was very nervous of purchasing my first boat and I realised I need not have been, we also made and learned from our mistakes. I decided to write this book for many reasons, but one was so that people can see how easy it is to purchase their first boat, and how simple it is to go through all the different things associated with it from launching your boat into the water to getting your boat a safety certificate.

In the following chapters I am going to take you through our canal boat journey from purchase to finished build. I also wanted a log of all we went through as a family and a record of Billy's unique achievements, so in years to come we could look back on it. The other reason for writing, was that we were lucky enough to have the amazing experience of being on George Clarkes Amazing Spaces, but, really the main reason why I started my book was because I was terrified of getting a boat, particularly being a single mum without a man about to help, support and provide the physical strength!

I wanted to write this book, so that other people can see that with a bit of determination and a dash of throwing caution to the wind you too can live the dream, so here we go, this is the story of our journey as a family with our first boat; MatildaJayne, enjoy!

Even though Billy was still only 17 years old he was already an award-winning carpenter, Billy had been bullied at school and the head of school blamed him. She spouted the usual rubbish that they 'have a zero tolerance to bullying,' it didn't appear that way to me, I believe, she just didn't want it to be shown on her OFSTED report, so it was easier for her to blame Billy. I took Billy away from all the trouble at school and home educated him. Later, after Billy had left the school, the bully admitted to Police that he had indeed bullied Billy. After the bully left school the following year, he attended the same college as Billy and he started to bully him there. The difference was the college took a more logical approach and investigated it thoroughly and they were having none of it. The bullying stopped immediately, and Billy was never bullied again. Billy was then left in peace to do what he went to college to do; learn.

The saying 'every cloud has a silver lining', definitely fits our situation, out of something bad something good has surfaced, had Billy not been bullied, had the head of the school been more supportive, Billy would not have achieved what he has today. The best thing I did was home educate Billy and send him to college at 14 years old. By the time Billy was 16 years old he was a qualified carpenter and had already won the Skillbuild competition, a prestigious event for people in the construction trade. At 15 years old he was the youngest person to fully transform an old horsebox into a camper van without ANY help. Not only did he plan the whole build himself, he re-designed the horse box into a fully functioning camper van, then he re-built the engine, fitted the electrics and all the plumbing, and he installed the heating all by himself, he did it to such a high standard even George Clarke was astounded.

Anyway, back to the refurbishing of the boat and another fine mess that Billy got me into! Billy is not only an expert carpenter he's an expert at wrapping me around his little finger, in fact as superb as he is at carpentry it's a tossup at which he is best at; carpentry or wrapping me round his little finger! So, it wasn't long;

half an hour to be precise that he had successfully convinced me I couldn't be without a narrow boat and within moments he had me trawling the internet looking for a suitable boat.

That's when we realised, we did not stand a cat in hells chance of getting one, they were a fortune, we couldn't find anything under £12,000 and they were all in various states of disrepair. Our dream or should I say Billy's soon came to an abrupt halt. A bit downhearted we started the wagon and limped home, bottom lips well and truly out. I should have known my son better and a mere 12 grand wasn't going to scupper his plans, a boat he wanted and a boat we were going to get.

My daughter, Matilda is a keen walker, but Billy is rubbish at walking for any period of time, he always has been, as a child I would have to drag him the few hundred yards from work to home, he was the laziest walker ever and that reluctance to use his legs for anything that was not absolutely necessary stayed with him as he grew up. Suddenly though walking was on the daily agenda and guess where we were to walk, yeah you got it, we were going for a walk down the canal. So, we all set off on our ulterior motive jaunt down the canal and we ended up at Galgate Marina, Billy immediately wanted to peruse the boats in the harbour. We trundled around for a while, eyeing up every boat and commenting as you do, then all three of us stopped dead in our tracks, our eyes transfixed on the one thing in front of us, the gleaming red boat that was sitting bobbing on the water and guess what? It had a large for sale sign on it with a mobile number to contact but they had not stated a price. I stood there dreaming, I was cocooned in my own little cartoon bubble, you know one of those things that are drawn over the characters head when they are deep in thought. I imagined myself cooking tea on my Rayburn whilst we gently bobbed up and down on the water. We would be moored out in the country in the middle of nowhere, the only noise being the wildlife passing by, or an insistent swan that was not leaving until it was fed. We would be far away from the madding crowd, no people shouting and moaning, no impatient drivers, no traffic wardens dictating where you park and no unnecessary traffic lights, no Police or people in authority watching your every move, just simple tranquillity.

My thoughts erupted like a volcano and after about 30 seconds my mind had successfully purchased the boat, we now owned her, and we were cruising out of the marina on our first journey and, knowing my Billy, his thought process would be very similar. Then the nagging began, it was in both ears, a kid at each side screeching into my poor ears. Both chanting in unison, working like a team, Orcas circling their prey, until it finally realises its fight with life is fruitless and sacrifices itself to its fate.

Billy being older, and the more accomplished nagger quickly changed tactics, after they have worn you down with noise levels registering dangerously high in the decibel scale, he then slumped to a silent, soothing whisper and looks at you with drooping, puppy dog eyes. Amazingly your now so happy with the peace you inadvertently succumb to his demands, kids are masters at getting what they want! He manages to turn it round so you think it's him that's doing you the favour, it's genius. Matilda, a little less experienced, had let her emotions run away with her and was now jumping up and down like a caged Chimpanzee, the fact we had no money fell on deaf ears and the nagging was building with a crescendo of epic proportions.

I didn't want to ring, I despise time wasters myself, I have been in business sales for many years and I had sold numerous things and my biggest bugbear was and is timewasters. I certainly did not want to be telephoning someone, giving them false hope of selling their pride and joy when we didn't have a pot to pee in. However, Billy had been so persistent in his continual nagging he had ground me down and I had lost the will to live and like a divvy I telephoned the number.

£36,000!!!!! It couldn't be, what for a boat?

The owner carried on saying we would be lucky to get one for less than £15,000 for the size we wanted. Chances are that it would be in a very poor condition for that price. Thankfully the owner was not concerned that we were fully-fledged award-winning time wasters and he chatted away quite happily advising me on the best way forward, even, knowing I was the proverbial time waster. After chatting for some time, I thanked him and broke the bad news to the kids. Billy was totally unfazed and said we just had to think smaller.

Of course, it would have been ideal for us to purchase a 40ft narrow boat, this would have given us enough space for the three of us to be comfortable in and it also would not be too long for me to manoeuvre as I had never driven a boat before and was absolutely terrified at the thought of it! Realistically though Billy was right, we just needed to get a foot on the ladder and get a boat, we could always save up and go bigger later.

We climbed up the steps out of the marina back to Vera, Matilda was already sitting in the cab, her bottom lip trembling, a tear rolled down her face and when she turned to look at me her face said it all, 'bad mummy,' together they had successfully turned this round and now it was my duty as a parent to get a boat, their team work was meritorious.

We set off home and yet again we went back to the drawing board, we reached home boat less. In the mean time I tried to get as much money together as I could, I went to the bank to see how much I could borrow and the kids grovelled unapologetically and with no shame to their Grandma for the next few weeks, when all combined together we got to about £11,000 and we trawled the internet looking for a suitable boat within our bargain basement price range.

There was very little for that price but eventually we found a boat, the only problem being, it was only 28ft long, beggars can't be choosers though, so we went to have a look. It was just much too small for the three of us, but the kids nagged, and Matilda immediately fell in love with her, within minutes she had picked out where her room would be situated, the size of which would not be much bigger than a postage stamp. The boat went to auction and we bid up to our £11,000, we did not win, and she went for £16,000 and she needed an awful lot of work!

We started to get more desperate and we started looking at anything and everything within our budget, we even drove all the way to Wales, Billy was actually quite happy to set off back in the boat cruising up the canal all the way from Wales as soon as we purchased it, the only thing is IF we got it, he'd never driven a boat, we also had no provisions with us and we live near Lancaster! At 4 miles an hour, even if everything went well, when would he have got home? This did not deter him however, and he would have set off regardless of the consequences. On arriving in Wales, we found the marina and asked a group of boat owners who were sitting outside barbecuing, directions to the boat for sale, after the howls of laughter had subsided to a muffled childish giggle, one of the men pointed us in the direction of the boat.

Their hysterical response when we asked about the boat did not raise our hopes of finding this boat as our hidden gem. We followed their directions and we walked around the corner, to see a mixture of rust and matt black paint, covering a rectangle which surprisingly was still floating. We entered the boat and it was clear who ever had been in it enjoyed sampling the various drugs Britain had to offer rather than the various canals. I wouldn't have let a rat live in it, the smell was putrid, and I just could not wait to leave. We immediately set off home, our dreams shattered, this time even Billy thought it was not meant to be, we just had to accept we had to save up and probably leave it until next year, we went home forgot our dream of being on the waterways and got on with life.

Nothing more was said about the boat, then one day I was pottering about in the garden, it must have been about a week later and my telephone rang and on the other end of the line was a voice saying, "you rang about my boat a while back do you remember?" It was the man that I had rung about the £36,000 boat, he explained he knew of an old boat needing to be sold quickly.

Jayne Walden

The person that owned the boat had died and the relatives lived abroad, they were keen to just get rid of the boat, it was moored at a Marina and the mooring fees were having to be paid by them. My eyes lit up and I just knew this was meant to be. He carried on the conversation explaining that the boat would basically need gutting and that it did not have a safety certificate. Not having a safety certificate was an immense concern for me and I had visions of this meaning it was not even fit to sail on the waterway. The safety certificate is not as scary as it sounds.

The Boat Safety Scheme or BSS is owned by the Canal & River Trust and the Environment Agency. It was set up to reduce the risk of boat fires, explosions or pollution harming anyone on the waterways. All narrow boats need to have an up to date Boat Safety Certificate. This is equivalent to a cars MOT certificate. A fully qualified examiner will inspect your boat and if it passes all the requirements set out it will be given a Boat Safety Scheme Certificate, which is valid for four years. Ours cost £167 for the examination and certificate. I rang the examiner who was happy to talk me through what I needed, which included vents, fire extinguishers, a fire blanket etc. It's fool proof and no need to be terrified if a boat is advertised without a certificate, have a good look into it, it may have just been in dry dock and someone has not bothered for whatever reason to renew it.

I chatted on the telephone and arranged to meet the salesman. I then raced out of the house to find the kids and tell them the great news, they were ecstatic. We set off in Vera to the marina and as we entered through the gateway, sitting on the water was the most beautiful boat I had ever seen. She was totally dilapidated, a ghastly green with an even ghastlier blue canopy but oozing with character, this was no super model boat, but perfection is boring, like the ugly duckling that transformed into the stunning swan this was our ugly duckling and from the moment I laid eyes on her I knew she was ours, not some daft mind playing illusion, this was for real we were having her, I turned to look at the kids and I immediately knew our thoughts were in unison, we were in love.

We raced over to the boat and we were met by the salesman, the kids could get away with their joyous childish excitement because they were kids! I think the salesman was a bit surprised that the nearing middle-aged mother was jumping about like she was attached to a pogo stick as well.

The salesman let us into the boat and even though we knew it was not in good condition and we had been forewarned, it was surprising just how bad it was. The whole inside of the boat was covered in a thick layer of grease, MDF was everywhere and I think Matilda and I could have done a better job of building the bedrooms and the kitchen. We were later to find out that whoever built it was obsessed with sealant, which just happened to be the strongest sealant ever, you could have nearly re-plated the boat with it. Sealant was everywhere, there were very few nails or screws, everything was held together with sealant, but I didn't care I loved her. I turned to Billy and his expression said a thousand words, he didn't have to speak I knew he felt the same way as me. I'll have her I said, the salesman said, "do you not want to check her over?" I didn't, I knew we would have to gut her so if she wasn't going to sink anything else was totally irrelevant.

Matilda jumping for joy when we first found MatildaJayne

Jayne Walden

◆ ◆ ◆

I had made buying a boat more difficult as I had narrowed our criteria for buying one. I was terrified of buying anything that was in dry dock. This was all new to me and I just could not imagine how a boat that size would be lifted out of the water or transported, I mean a narrow boat trundling down the road on the back of a lorry isn't an everyday sight! Again, I was wrong, I could not believe how simple it was and it wasn't overly expensive either. If I was to buy again, I would not be concerned about buying a boat in dry dock, that would have opened so many more buying possibilities.

I was advised by the salesman to get a survey prior to purchase, the boat would have to be lifted out of the water, so this could be completed. I contacted a surveyor and there were different prices dependent on what you wanted doing. As we knew the boat needed totally gutting, I just wanted the basic survey which was about £200. I just needed to know the boat was not going to sink, basically the metal was thick enough with no weak points. I arranged with the marina to have the boat lifted, which is basically it gets lifted by a crane with the boat in a cradle so that the surveyor can easily check all round it. I booked the surveyor.

The men at the marina must have thought we were the strangest family going. We were beyond excited, and I was not afraid to let anyone know it, Billy kept giving me that knowing look, he didn't have to say what he thought; it was 'mum stop it! Your such an embarrassment!' Matilda couldn't have cared less and joined in the frivolities although she did have the excuse that she was only 8 yrs old!

After the survey is completed it then can either be put back in the water or put on the ground into dry dock. At this point we just presumed it would pass and the boat would be put on the ground in preparation for the transporter.

I waited patiently for the call from the surveyor, it came as quite a shock when he rang and told me it had failed the surveyors report. Clearly, we were all upset, and we believed that was the end of our dream, we couldn't afford to buy her. She needed re-plating and not only was this thousands of pounds, she would have to be transported to and from the platers, so with this added onto the price, when we added it up altogether the total amount made her far too expensive. We were complete boat novices and just presumed she would be okay, she was floating what could be wrong?

We found out from the surveyor that the metal had to be a certain thickness and in parts it was too thin, had we hit something in the water the metal could have ruptured, even if we did take the risk how could we move her? There are 7 locks out of the Marina and I had never even started a boat never mind negotiated a lock, we were sure to hit something. So, we couldn't even move her without added expense as well as save up for the plating the risk was too high, so some things are just not meant to be or, so I thought.

We accepted our fate and headed out of the Marina, all sad and forlorn, like we'd had a bereavement, it was a damn boat, man up I thought as Matilda's face was streaming with so many tears, she was in danger of flooding the Marina!

We accepted for the second time, the realisation that we were not going to get a boat, we kept an eye open looking on the internet, but we did not let it worry us or consume our lives. Our adventure had just begun. You get knocked down, but you get up again. We contemplated a cruiser, just to get started, but we were not keen and decided just to keep saving up. I need not have worried as it was not long until the phone rang again, it was the salesman from the Marina he had spoken to the owners of the boat and they had said they would pay for the plating if I paid for the lifting and transport. This amount was to be deducted from the original asking price. I could not believe our luck. I immediately accepted their offer, I snapped their hands off and raced to the inform the kids of the great news.

Jayne Walden

Our YouTube link for the replating lift
https://youtu.be/kzJH21ywhEc
You tube username = matildariver1

◆ ◆ ◆

We arranged with the marina for the boat to be lifted again and headed back to the marina to wait patiently for the transporter to arrive, we were amazed when a normal HGV truck, drove into the yard. I was expecting some wide load outfit with an escort van in front with flashing lights, warning every one of the impending massive load coming towards them. Instead they lifted the boat up and popped her onto a couple of railway sleepers and few straps were thrown over her to secure her to the trailer and she was ready for transportation. My hysterical concerns of not being able to move the boat and that it was going to be a massive task was unfounded.

The lorry driver of course didn't share our childish enthusiasm and excitement about our new purchase. In fact, I really admired him for being able to meet a customer, load a boat onto his trailer and then take the boat to the customers preferred destination without uttering a single word! Either he was beyond excited and was gob smacked and couldn't talk, or he was a miserable grumpy beggar, I think it was the latter, but we didn't care if he got it to the platers, his persona was irrelevant. Once the boat was loaded, which was a remarkably easy feat as it shows on the YouTube video, the lorry left the marina and we jumped in Vera to follow the transporter to the platers, camera in tow, recording every moment.

The platers were more understanding they let us relish in the glory of our new purchase. MatildaJayne was lifted from the lorry by 4 fork lift trucks, I was a little concerned at this point as there was no professional crane and cradle like at the marina. I watched very nervously as our precious boat was in the air on the forks of four trucks. She was thankfully placed safely down ready for the whole of her underside to be re-plated which consisted of putting in place and welding sheets of metal all around the hull (the part that would be in the water).

It took a few weeks for her to be replated and it was arranged for us to meet the transporter at the marina for us to take control of our boat, now remember we are boat virgins, and this was the most daunting experience for me ever.

The transport pulled up with the same recalcitrant driver, who had already managed the inconceivable feat of being able to take a full boat from his lorry and trailer with no communication whatsoever not even a grunt, it was admirable really, I could imagine Simon Cowell introducing him on Britain's got talent, it certainly made Billy and I giggle trying to draw him into making conversation, but, he was a genius mute and was having none of it. Anyway, the main thing was the boat arrived safely, undamaged and on time and for a pretty reasonable price, so I had no complaints, we just accepted that there were no pleasantries whatsoever, perhaps therefore this transportation company was so reasonably priced, and it added a bit of humour to the journey.

The hull is blacked to protect the bottom section of the boat, so specifically the area of the boat that is in the water and just above the water line. The "blacking" process protects the hull from rust, pitting, rubbing (through locks, other boats, banks etc) and generally extends the life of the hull. The general upkeep of a narrow boat means that you need to carry out certain maintenance jobs and blacking is amongst those jobs. Some maintenance work you will be able to do yourself, however blacking your narrow boat can be quite time consuming and very difficult whilst in the water.

After a few weeks we returned to watch our boat being placed back on a trailer to go off to the new marina we were launching from. They craned her up again and there she was hanging, ready to be put in the water. It's a negative moment for every novice boat owner to surface from their boat and these 'know it all types' who were just watching from the sides, to put their opinion forward unconcerned or not of whether you want to hear it. The doom and gloom that we heard when they found out that we had never driven a boat before was so depressing.

We, well when I say we, I mean Billy, had to drive a boat a few hundred yards out of a marina and onto the canal, a boat that at full speed does 4 miles an hour. Obviously when we set off it was not going to launch at full speed, galloping off like a bolting horse as soon as we turned the engine over.

How hard can it be to drive a boat, and if things went so drastically wrong, as we were told in no uncertain terms, by fellow boaters, that it was certain to go wrong, and that my totally incompetent son was destined to crash, did they not think that he would not just turn the engine off and I push it away from its impending doom? So, we ignored the baying crowd, incidentally none of whom offered to help and navigate the boat out of the marina for us.

They seemed experienced enough to comment but not to take the helm, had any one of them driven our boat out with their words we would have gracefully departed the marina like the dancer Darcy Bussell.

I need not have worried about the launch though, the men at the marina took over everything, they just popped our boat in the water and it was such a simple task. The pleasant thing was they did not rush us, we could enjoy the moment. It's a job to them but it's an adventure and a hobby for us, so we wanted to record every moment. They waited patiently whilst we loaded our bits and bobs out of our camper van Vera and allowed us to park Vera at the marina until a friend could run us back to pick her up. We all wanted to experience our first journey on the boat together.

The men then directed us out of the Marina and helped us negotiate the boat past the other boats, Billy expertly directed our new purchase like he had been driving one all his life and as he was still only 16 years old. We turned right out of the marina and headed up the Lancaster canal to our new destination, broad smiles plastered to our faces and grinning from ear to ear.

We thought we knew the boating etiquette, I didn't know at this point how wrong I was, and I had impressed upon Billy the correct way to pass other boats he convinced me he did and after I had asked him a handful of times he became quite stroppy telling me to shut up and he had everything under control.

Our first journey was to Galgate, where we were mooring next to a friend for the first week. Billy was stood at the stern as happy as a pig in clover and Matilda and I sat at the front loving every minute just looking out. The first boat came the other way which put me into a blind panic and unfortunately for Billy he was meeting it at a bridge, but as cool as cucumber he expertly manoeuvred the boat round, dealing with the bridge and the oncoming boat, however the other boater didn't seem to know what he was doing. We slowed down, moved over and gave way to him, so we were a bit disappointed when rather than politely thanking us he glared and trundled off in his boat, how rude I thought, and we set off again.

The next boat we met was a very small cruiser, it appeared quite dilapidated and we slowed to pass, there it was bobbing about in front of us like a cork, they looked a certain type, a bit judgemental I know, we just thought they were stoned and too out of it to drive properly. Matilda and I commented to each other about how they were a bit bonkers on the canal and clearly could not drive.

As the next boat came, I warned Billy and he again moved over to the left to pass as if in a car, the 65ft oncoming boat kept coming for us and the dual began, the only difference being this had not been prearranged and there had been no accepted code of procedure discussed beforehand. The truth was we were totally in the wrong and the poor bloke in the other boat didn't have a clue what we were doing. As he swerved to the side, this way and that, his eyes shot daggers at me, I started to have an inkling that my son just might be in the wrong, and that we were in fact passing on the incorrect side. I politely asked the passing boater if we were passing on the correct side, "NO" he said in a very disgruntled tone and cruised on.

Oh dear! I went to Billy and explained that the reason why everybody glared at us was not because people were either incompetent or stoned, it was because we were passing on the wrong side and the man in the cruiser who had acted as if he was stoned was just terrified.

Billy's answer to this was "Well that's what the woman in the carpet shop told me," "WHAT," I said in a very load voice, Billy then went on to inform me that when we had picked Matilda's bedroom carpet up he had asked the lady in the carpet shop which side they passed and she had said the same as on the road. I did ask him why he had not thought to ask the men at the marina rather than a carpet fitter about boat etiquette, but it kind of fell on deaf ears as he stuck his nose in the air doing his best Kenneth Williams impression and then managed to totally divert away from his mistake by saying I had to leave him as he had to concentrate on his steering.

I returned to Matilda at the front of the boat and we both laughed as I explained to her what Billy had done. After we had got safely to our destination Billy joined in the merriment.

We moored our boat just outside Galgate and this was to be our first night on the water it was very exciting, we knew we had done the right thing buying MatildaJayne whom we had already fallen for hook line and sinker.

Everything was a new experience, we had never even tied a boat up before, to this day we haven't got the lingo and there will be correct terminology for tying a boat up I'm sure. At this point long time and professional boaters will be tutting at me whilst they read this! I suppose I could have looked on the internet and found the correct terminology for everything narrow boat related, but I think that would have ruined the book.

The whole idea of this is to prove you don't have to be an expert or think you own the canal system to get going, you can just get a boat and get on with it so if any expert is unhappy with what or how I say it sorry but tough!

I found the last bit of our initial journey the scariest, the bit that you must jump off.

Now, I'm no sissy, prior to helping my son my main job was remedying problem horses, I have raced at Market Rasen racecourse, one of the most challenging in the country, and I have won at Musselborough races, so not wanting to blow my own trumpet but, travelling at speed and approaching 5ft fences at 35 miles an hour is not a concern of mine.

This was different though, the horse was jumping I was merely sat on top of it and you know what they say, 'a loose horse rarely falls,' so as a jockey I tend to let the horse do what it does best, especially if we did get onto trouble. When a horse has planned something, they don't need someone riving on their mouths trying to interfere. The difference here it was me jumping and I was making the decision, I wasn't a brave and gallant thoroughbred, bred to leap and spurred on with my animal instinct to race with a herd. I was a n approaching middle age dumpy woman, with the responsibility of being the sole provider of two kids and I was approaching unknown territory at 4 miles an hour and was expected to leap into or onto the unknown.

With this approaching trauma on my shoulders I had the added disadvantage of some bossy bloke at the helm screaming jump, screeching at the top of his voice and seemingly sounding like he was warming up for the fastest talker competition. I couldn't get my legs to move, my mind was willing, but the body was not, every time I went to jump, I teetered on the edge then an imaginary force pulled me back, onto the safety of the boat.

I was stood on the edge wavering to and fro, I had managed to pull off that perfect dance move of Michael Jacksons, you know in his video for Thriller where they all lean forward, feet flat to the ground and defy gravity, I have heard that their shoes were glued to the ground but I don't know. Forget years of training to be a dancer and maybe a bit of cheating, you can get the same effect when your expected to jump from a narrow boat at 4 miles an hour. So, as my body and mind argued it out like an old married couple sick of the sight of each other, we eventually hit the banking, thank goodness for buoys which softened the blow. Billy was screaming "mum" like a banshee and I was screaming back that he was going too fast and I could not jump. As the boat was safely wedged in the embankment its bottom stuck out in the middle of the canal I leapt off, rather proudly thinking I looked like a gazelle and held the rope as if I was holding a naughty horse that was going to bolt off and I was having none of it.

Billy then had the task of getting the back-end round and he did that with incredible ease. He then jumped off giving me that knowing look and secured the boat to the embankment, after he got up and stood straight, he turned and looked at me, I smiled as if absolutely nothing had happened and said, "Should I put the kettle on,"

CHAPTER 3

APPLYING TO BE ON AMAZING SPACES

◆ ◆ ◆

My initial application to go on George Clarke's Amazing Spaces was a bit of a flop to say the least. I applied, because Billy had converted an old worn out horsebox, on a Volkswagen LT35 chassis, that we now lovingly call Veronica, into a functioning camper van while he was only 15 years old; I thought this achievement would be a good story to go on the programme.

I don't know where he got that idea from, but it was the start of things to come. This was his first big build. Billy chose the build as we already had Vera, which when we bought her, was also a horsebox. When I finished with her for that use, we drove 3 hrs down to a scrap yard to buy an old body off an LDV Convoy, and at 14 years old, in the middle of the scrap yard Billy put the body on Vera's chassis cab.

Billy is a very handy lad to have around and can do most things himself he just gets on with it. He was friendly with a local mechanic at the time near our horse yard, he had advised us not to buy Vera under any circumstances and that Volkswagen LT's were generally a pile of junk. Billy having very little mechanical knowledge at the time agreed with his much older friend. I didn't, as I was not impressed with his friends' mechanical abilities and neither was Billy as he matured and learnt more, went on to assist at a 'proper' garage in Lancaster.

So, I ignored the 'mechanic' and bought her. We drove her home and boy was she slow and then 3 miles from home the temperature light came on and I was a bit worried. We got home, and I rang the local mobile mechanic and he stopped off on his way home, I feared the worst, but it was only a £2.98 fan belt, and the reason for the sluggishness? A bird's nest in her air filter!

Once sorted we never looked back, Vera has been everywhere, she went to France in boiling heat when new cars were at the side of the road overheating, she stayed a constant just under half on the temperature gauge, she pulls the rally car and trailer for fun and has never once broken down, she is the best vehicle I ever bought and the mechanic who operates not far from our yard, I've never let him have his hands on her hence why she is still running! So, we had had experience of the Volkswagen LT and that's why we bought another in the shape of Veronica.

Veronica when we picked her up

Billy did the whole build of Veronica himself, the only thing I did was make the curtains! Billy did everything else, from changing the cam-belt and replacing the brakes and getting it prepared for her M.O.T, to fitting a new floor, removing the old very heavy ramp to fitting the electrics. To this day I do not know how a 15-year-old managed to remove that heavy ramp with thick strongly supressed springs all by himself.

Taking the ramp off.

I thought that the refurbishment of Veronica alone had been a fantastic achievement for an adult never mind a child, therefore the full refurbishment of a boat by Billy might be interesting television and reading.

Our first trip out in the finished Veronica

So, I thought it would be a breeze to get onto Amazing Spaces and sent off my email to apply. Soon after the email had landed a lady contacted me and said that she was interested in Billy's story, what I did not realise is that she was freelance, and as I was to find out, was not committed to Amazing Spaces for long nor committed to maintaining their good reputation and I believed she messed us about. This lady failed to explain the usual process. I later found out that the freelance researchers source the people they think would be good for the programme, usually made a short recording with them and gave it to the programme producer to decide if they were suitable for the programme.

The woman who had approached us never explained any of this to us and whilst Billy was still only a child, he was very excited at the prospect of meeting George and going on the show.

In my opinion, this lady did very little work, after all she didn't have to, she had Billy and I running around doing the work for her. As Billy was excited at the chance of being on the programme we did as she asked. She rang or emailed with multiple demands. We never actually even met her, never did any filming of us herself. She did however call relentlessly or email asking for me to do more and more filming of Billy.

I did this and kept sending the film over to her, but, never happy with it and would ask for more. Repeatedly sent the same questions in a different format. I think this might have worn anyone out and I was getting tired with it, it had become quite tedious. Then she wouldn't message for weeks then she would contact asking for the answers to a list of questions which had been answered previously.

We then heard nothing, so a few months later I contacted her, where upon she said we were not successful. She hadn't even had the decency to contact us tell us she just kept us waiting, even after she had put us through months of questions and filming. We were obviously disappointed but also annoyed and felt our time was completely wasted. We thought nothing more of it and got on with our lives.

Then one day I received an email from Amazing Spaces asking if we were going to do anything else and what we were up too. You can imagine my response it was curt to say the least, I put that if a camper built solely by a 15-year-old was not good enough for them, what could be, and that if Billy was ever to refurbish a rocket I would be in touch. I even put that maybe George was jealous of Billy! Oh dear. I sent it and laughed away to myself, I told Billy and he wasn't bothered that I had responded in the way I did. I asked him if he thought I may have scuppered his chances of going on, but he said he felt deflated the way he was treated last time and didn't want to go through that process again, I agreed, so, we had a giggle to ourselves and life went on as normal.

I could understand if the staff with the show were a bit annoyed with me, and I thought I would never hear from anyone again, so imagine my surprise when the phone rang almost immediately.

A woman spoke on the other end of the telephone and she

explained the previous lady was freelance and didn't work for Amazing Spaces and that she had left. She went onto say that she was not like her and certainly would not act in that way, and if the build went ahead the experience would be different.

I could tell this person was totally professional and a different kettle of fish, so we had a laugh about the email, (which at this point I was very embarrassed about and wanted the ground to swallow me up); but at least I had explained the reason for my poor attitude and rude response.

She then started to ask about the important thing; Billy's project, she asked me what he was going to do, and I proceeded to tell her all about it. She said that it sounded great and that someone would be in touch to do what they call a recce, which is a pre-filming visit to determine its suitability for shooting and that this was to be filmed. This was already a vast improvement on last time and sounded far more professional as the previous woman just wanted us to film ourselves.

It was all very real and exciting at this point we started really looking forward to the experience. We were a bit apprehensive and nervous, particularly after what we had been through. My other worry was Matilda, as much as I love her, she is autistic, and tends to say it as it is. I was a little worried that she would take over and detract from the purpose of the film, which was Billy and his carpentry skills. When filming began, as predicted Matilda did take over and bossed people about relentlessly, the film crew loved her particularly the female director who Matilda absolutely worshipped after about 3 minutes of meeting her.

It was the 15th May 2018 when we had our first face to face with someone from Spaces, he was one of the camera men and a senior researcher. At this point the boat was moored in the countryside, away from the roadside, so sat nav details were difficult, so, I agreed a place to meet him and then walked down to the boat with him. I presumed he would be carrying heavy camera equipment, so I thought I could give him a hand to carry it all to the boat. He was getting out of the car when I arrived at our meeting point, hauling bags of equipment out of the boot, we did the normal meet and greet, and set off down the canal path to the boat.

He was very friendly and laid back and immediately put Billy at ease who was terrified of being filmed. When we arrived at the boat, he introduced himself and initially questioned Billy about the build he was going to do. Matilda was jumping up and down doing her usual impression of a caged chimpanzee demanding attention. He informed Matilda that she would get her turn in time. Matilda however, had her impatient head on and was having none of this, she was convinced she should be the star of the show and nobody, but nobody, was going to tell her any different. He tried to shake her off like one of those annoying dogs that just will not stop sniffing you, he then launched himself into the boat with Billy in tow and tried to get on with the job in question.

I did as I was told, I thought one of us better to save the guys nerves from being shredded. So, I sat outside waiting patiently doing my best to try to control Matilda who was trying every trick in the book to try and get into camera shot. It was clear she was never going to understand that if you walked in front of the camera it did not automatically mean you would be on the telly. Matilda and Billy were like chalk and cheese, one, Matilda, was like a celebrity that would do anything to get in shot, someone who would attend the opening of an envelope if it guaranteed some media coverage. The other, Billy, the camera man was struggling to get to look at the camera lens, but he persevered filming Billy with an ever-persistent small girl relentlessly bobbing her head in and out of camera shot, photo bombing for England.

In the meantime, Billy was relentlessly making excuses not to be on film, he was happy with his hands in shot holding the tools, but that was about it, he was adamant he did not want to talk to camera. The guy explained that it would be difficult for him to film an episode of Amazing Spaces not only in silence but also not featuring the person who was doing the build. Obviously as adults we knew the dynamics of Billy not being on film and that it would just not work, but Billy carried on regardless thinking he could pull this baby off, the cameraman was just as steadfast saying he would not budge and as he relentlessly filmed Billy's every move and word.

So, he managed to convince Billy and a very shaky and nervous child started to explain what he was doing, even if it did include various interludes of "Was that alright" from Billy who was seeking reassurance at every opportunity.

I, on the other hand was the pushy mother, telling him to get on with it and not to be so silly and everything was going to be fine, until it came to my turn and my emotions were a mirror image of Billy's but, that was different, that was me!

Billy awkwardly relaxed into it. After an hour or so, Billy had found his feet and was happily chatting camera his shyness and awkwardness diminishing with every minute and his cheeky character started to shine through.

Matilda, who I explained is a totally different kettle of fish, was still being boisterous, cheeky and she had totally omitted the shyness queue. Even though the cameraman had a job to do he was the ultimate professional and took it all in his stride. He warmed to Matilda immediately and she came across brilliantly on camera. She would nonchalantly walk past in the back ground, she constantly needed 'the toilet'! Then there was every excuse under the sun to go on the boat as he was filming Billy, I again tried to explain to her that just because she walked in shot did not mean they would use the footage and would probably not use the footage if she just appeared in shot. Explaining this fell on deaf ears and she was adamant to get in shot. I found her behaviour hilarious and I had to stifle my giggles, I didn't want to knock Billy off track, nor be heard on camera or exacerbate the excitement of an already hyperactive Matilda.

The recce lasted a few hours and then he explained that he had what he needed, we walked him back to his car and said our goodbyes, then the waiting game began.

We walked back to the boat and we did what I think anyone would we trawled through every bit in our heads and constantly asked each other questions and searched for reassurance. You know how it is, if you say it over and over again it makes it okay; 'Do you think I looked silly when I said such and such on camera,' You really want the world to swallow you up, but that isn't going to happen so you think if you relentlessly keep mentioning it, it will go away. People are just going to agree you didn't sound like a divvy, not because they agree you didn't but because they are sick of you constantly drivelling on and hope if they agree you will just shut up!

We went on and on, constantly evaluating, what we did right what we did wrong, Billy the eternal pessimist, did not think things had gone well and had decided it just was not going to happen. My argument of why someone of the cameraman's filming calibre would carry on regardless for 3 hours if we were rubbish was not acknowledged and Billy carried on quite happily with his negative journey back to the boat.

We had to just draw a line under it or wondering and surmising would have eaten us alive and we would have been on the brink of a break down. So, we carried on with our daily routines and little was mentioned of George and Amazing Spaces. We all secretly thought about it, and, if the thought became too rampant in Matilda's head and it managed to creep out into a vocal expression, it was quickly shot down and quietened and it wasn't spoken about; we had to do this for mental self-preservation. Hours became days. days became weeks, and even me, ever the optimist was convinced we had not been chosen.

We accepted we were not going to be on the programme and never thought any more of it. Then one day we were driving, taking a vehicle to the local garage and the phone rang, it was the researcher/cameraman, he asked if we had started the build, which we hadn't, he then asked if we could put it on hold for a couple more weeks, so it could be passed by the series producer. He told us that this still was still not a yes to go ahead, but obviously we knew that it was very positive news. We were then on edge waiting for the producer to decide, it felt like an eternity waiting and now we had got this far we really wanted to be on the programme. Eventually the call came, I was walking around the quietest shop ever with other people walking round the shop. You know what it's like and I've done it myself, your somewhere where a phone going off is just not okay. The other people glared at me like we were at a funeral. You could see the annoyed glances and feel the tuts as their expressions said a thousand words, honestly can she not be off that thing for 1 minute. The funny thing is I hate seeing people glued to their phones, especially kids, there is so much more to life, it's so sad, I won't even let Matilda have a phone. I'd had mine glued to me for the previous few weeks, good or bad news I wasn't going to miss that call, I just needed to know immediately. It was the cameraman on the end of the line, he asked me how I was, and I, not wanting to be be rude I just wanted him to blurt it out whether we had been chosen or not. He didn't even need to say hello, I just needed to know the producer's decision.

Then the decision we'd been waiting for - we had the go ahead, the thing was though, I couldn't whoop or jump for joy or even scream with excitement as I was in a shop that made a church look like a rave so I said, "That's great" in the most quiet monotone voice without any intonation, he must of thought cheeky cow, I've gone through all this, got her on the show and she's about as excited as a vegetarian in a butchers. He then went on to talk about what would happen next, As I crept out of the shop my voice increasing in volume with every step and I inadvertently added more and more expression to my voice as the conversation went on. As soon as I was in the clear I had built it up to how excited I should have been when I spoke to him at the beginning of the conversation. He must have thought I was absolutely barking mad and been worried as he had just signed us to his very reputable programme!

CHAPTER 4

THE REAR CUT

◆ ◆ ◆

After stripping out MatildaJayne, we needed a plan, and that's both Billy and my Achilles Heel. I am the most impatient person in the world when it comes to building. Stand in a supermarket queue and I'm awesome at it, whilst you see people moaning and tutting, willing the person in front to just launch their shopping into a bag regardless of if it's a cream bun or something delicate, just so they can save a waiting customer a few seconds. I on the other hand just accept it and relax, things like that do not wind me up, but, if I'm going to build something I want to start yesterday.

I actually physically struggle to listen to a plan, with my facial movements I could have been Jim Careys' body double in The Mask, I sit there gurning ready to go, one slight slip of a word in the person who's instructing me, a pause for breath and I'm off like a bull in a china shop.

Billy on the other hand has the patience of a saint, if he gets something wrong, he'll go back to the start and start all over again, regardless of how many man hours he has put in. I don't, I'll spend another 4 days of wasting time trying to get it right, going around in a massive circle to rectify and cover up my mistakes, like a huge unnecessary sticking plaster. There is no way on this earth I am wasting the 4 hours it took me to get into the mess I'm in.

I'm the same with directions, if I believe that the sat nav is wrong I will defy it and set off in the direction I believe to be right. You try and turn me round not a chance, I'll go in a circle or U-turn down another road but I'm not wasting those miles I've done.

Even though Billy is patient, he's terrible at planning, he just seems to get on and do it and it always works, if he was not my son, I'd hate him! I hear the smarty pants of you going yeah, well one day it won't, well so be it worse things have happened. He may plan it in his head, I don't know, all I know is the poor cameraman had a nightmare trying to get a plan out of him. So, we all have our little idiosyncrasies and that's ours, neither of us can plan, or, should I say neither of us are willing to plan and one of us can't plan and I think you can see from the build which one is which.

Billy decided to cut the back of the boat out and get rid of the biggest job first, also the one that would make the most mess, there was no point doing anything else because this would obviously be damaged as we opened the whole boat to the elements. The only thing we had done was ballast the boat and put part of the floor down.

For obvious reasons the boat needed to be level, it did not have to be perfect as when we put things in this was clearly going to affect the balance of the boat unless we were very lucky and everything, we put in balanced with each side. So, we had to ballast it and put part of the floor in, it would have been hard work without a bit of flooring down and would have been more dangerous carrying things if you had to negotiate floor joists etc.

I was absolutely terrified about cutting the back of the boat out, it just seemed so extreme to me as it did not take anything to keep putting me off from starting. I trusted Billy implicitly, but he was still only a kid with no experience of cutting such thick metal, which was about 4mm thick and he certainly had no experience of it being in such an awkward position and part of the structure of a boat. He had to get the angle right and obviously get both sides to match. I would not have even dared to attempt it, but Billy had no concerns what so ever and happily measured it out ready to be cut.

The rear cut was one of the things the programme was desperate to get on film, so the film crew arrived and filmed Billy's every move, at one point he even had a camera attached to the angle grinder. Billy still managed to do a perfect job under the pressure of being filmed, the cameraman had to get it right first time, as once cut if he missed it Billy couldn't cut it again.

The weight of the metal he cut out was incredible, even though the amount from the top of the roof did not look like a big piece. I had to stand out of the way, one reason was I did not want to distract Billy, and the other was the sparks from the angle grinder went quite a distance. It took Billy about 45 mins to cut it out and then I was called over to view. The change was substantial, it totally transformed the boat, I could not believe how much more open it looked I could have cried, Billy had pulled it off again.

We now had to work quickly as not only was the boat not water tight it was not secure. I had already collected the wood for the frame and Billy set to work building the frame for the back. Prior to changing the back Billy had had to stand up whilst driving the boat which is not relaxing especially over a long distance and how ever poor the weather was the canopy had to be down as the screen was plastic and not safe enough to see through clearly whilst driving.

The frame was made with 3 x 2 and 3 x 3 wood, he curved the beams of the roof for water to run off. Billy managed to get the frame made and in position in less than a day, but we were disagreeing about the roof and what to do with it. At least we had the frame up and we could now put a tarpaulin over it and that's what we did.

Security had become less of an issue as one day we saw a man strimming the other side of the canal and I started talking to him and telling him what we were doing and how time consuming it was having to carry all the materials down the canal to the boat and he said that we could moor on his private side of the canal. This was music to our ears as this meant we did not have to move every 14 days as the Canal and River Trust rules state, there seems to be no reasoning with them if you need longer for any reason.

We were now on private land and the owner allowed our Volkswagen LT Vera to drive on and we had made make shift beds in there so now we could stop overnight and keep a watch on the unsecure boat, looking back with such a short time span and having to hold some parts of the build off to work round the filming crews, other filming commitments, I don't think we would of finished the build without the support of the land owner who's kind gesture was invaluable.

So, this gave us a chance to endlessly row about what we were doing with the roof over the rear of the boat, Billy wanted a canvas roof to roll back, but I wanted a solid roof with a ladder up the side, so I could sit out on the top. Billy as usual won and that meant I had to find a suitable roll back roof, he said that I should get a Webasto one from a Volkswagen like the ones they have on the campers.

I thought this would be no problem, how wrong I was, there was no second-hand ones and the cheapest new one was £650. Not only was this out of our reach financially, but we were sticking to a budget for the programme and I think that's one of the best moments on Amazing Spaces, when people have done amazing builds for little money. When they source second hand items or make something else into something totally new for the job, they need it to do.

If I bought new, I felt like a failure. So, I had to use an alternative, I researched it and trawled the internet until I felt sick. I decided on using a MK1 Cortina convertible roof this was the largest I could get, it was not as big as I wanted so I was going to buy it and extend it. I found one, but he wanted £200 for it and would not budge, and it was 4 hrs away.

The auction ended in 5 days' time, so I waited to buy it. In the meantime, I periodically checked the internet for a VW folding roof really knowing I would never get one. Five days later I was sitting at the computer watching the minutes go down, ready to bid on the Cortina roof, it had 52 mins to go so I kept flicking about on the internet looking at other things. Then and this is Gods truth I looked and there, as a new listing, was a second-hand Volkswagen roll back roof for £100 it was meant to be, I immediately rang the number and set off on the hour and a half drive to collect it.

Billy wanted to make an aluminium frame to house the folding roof and he set about hammering and shaping sheets of aluminium. He had never worked with metal before and he did a superb job, it looked outstanding and is totally waterproof. He added guttering to the side, making the guttering by folding the sheet aluminium.

I sat in the back as he folded back the new roof, I looked up at the clear blue sky and beamed from ear to ear, Billy was right again it felt spacious, you were sitting in the open air, like an indoor patio, what a transformation from a grotty old canvas canopy.

The extension on the back transformed the whole boat, prior to this you stepped down to the kitchen which was tight, dark and claustrophobic, now, with the extension the kitchen could go at the back of the boat. We wanted to put a seating area at the back of the boat, but it also had to be a seat to drive from, the next bit was my brainwave and that was to use the rear seat from a car. We went to the local scrap yard and managed to get a leather seat out of an Audi A4 for £15! It looks awesome fitted, is really comfy and can just be wiped down I was over the moon with it.

The glass was a large expense, and for the front, which was not only a large size, but also an unusual shape it was going to be hundreds of pounds. We decided to have a go at cutting it ourselves and as you can see from the programme it was not an initial success as we quickly found out you cannot cut toughened glass!

If you're going to do a build and your amateurs like we were on most things you are going to make mistakes the difference was ours were caught on camera and put on national television.

Remember most people are supportive and if you don't try you never learn, learning from your mistakes is the best way. Everybody has detractors and critics that just cannot help but put forward their negative opinions, but I'll almost guarantee, these people are the ones who do nothing. The more successful you become the more the nasty comments come out and the green-eyed monster rears his ugly head. But if you want to get on you must ignore them, a brilliant quote by Sir Winston Churchill is:

You have enemies? Good. That means you've stood up for something, sometime in your life.

And this is true, if you sit at home doing nothing and never say anything, granted you won't have anyone say a wrong word about you, but can you honestly say you have lived your life?

So, we tried to do as much as we could do ourselves, regardless of the consequences. Paying for some glass and for someone to cut it was not going to be cheap and it was going to be over £1000 just for the glass, so again we had to improvise.

The windows we bought from the scrap yard, they came out of an old camper van, they worked out better as they were sliding so on a hot day you can open them all. The rest we cut ourselves, we made the front window into quarters and this was more aesthetically pleasing to the eye and I'm glad we did it this way.

After Billy's little faux pas with his first window that exploded into a million pieces over his Grandmas yard our skill improved and he cut and fitted all the windows himself, quite an achievement as the front window was an unusual shape and narrowed quite significantly in a short space, but again he managed and his job was superb and water tight.

After the back was completed our initial worry was it not being water tight and it didn't rain properly for ages, so we couldn't see if there was anywhere where it leaked. Then when it did rain, boy did it rain, and the wind drove the water in hard into the rear of the boat. We had two leaks albeit only very slight. Billy quickly realised it was a guttering and sealant problem and he rectified it and it never leaked again.

We were very happy after doing such a major change for the first time that this was the only teething problem we encountered. We were now well on our way to completing the build. We needed to be as George was coming in about a weeks' time. The only thing we were struggling with now was getting the paint on, in the hit and miss weather we were having.

◆ ◆ ◆

CHAPTER 5

THE BUILD

◆ ◆ ◆

I'll take you through the boat from the back to the front and what Billy did to transform it from the tired old girl she was to the super model stunner she is today. This photograph was taken when the boat had been lifted out at the marina ready to go for plating, it was strange to see underneath her but also exciting because this was the point when we knew our journey was for real, she was on the first steps to going to the canal ready for us to board to set off on our canal adventure.

As you can see the back of the boat was covered by an ugly and worn out canopy, this leaked water and was not secure. The whole of the space under the canopy was wasted and the previous owner had just stored a few things in there that could stand the wet.

MatildaJayne on the transport before re-plating

❖ ❖ ❖

Billy started by completely removing the canopy and the metal railings that surrounded it, the metal railings were not only the frame for the canopy, but they also acted as a guard rail for when you were driving the boat. You basically leaned on these as you steered the boat and they prevented people from falling in. We were astounded when we found out even these were held together by the dreaded sealant that had been used the whole way through the inside of the boat.

Even though the sealant was mega strong we never expected the metal frame to be sealed on with it, finding this out was beyond belief. Billy then went on to clear everything from inside the boat and it was amazing just how much stuff there was. We cleared out 4 loads with Vera, rotted or mouldy wood and MDF, she was jam packed.

There were though some things in the boat interior which were saleable. We managed to get a bit of money in return for quite a few items, we managed to sell the canopy, the fire and the shower, we even managed to sell the steps.

When Billy took the floor up the underneath had been ballasted with lead and concrete lintels, all of which we sold and managed to get a couple of hundred pounds for them, the money all went back into the build, it went towards buying other things for the boat, like the flooring.

I chose scaffolding board for the floor and Billy will admit that he thought I was barking mad. I love old wood and love recycling and using reclaimed items. So, I trawled the internet for some suitable wood. Now even though a narrowboat is narrow it's not that narrow and 45ft is quite long, so I knew this would be our biggest spend. I found some on the internet that I fell in love with, all the lengths were extremely long there were no nail holes, none of the boards were warped and I could not believe how cheap they were.

We only spent £500 on the wood for the whole floor, I believe that if we had gone and bought new wood from a builders' suppliers this amount could have been thousands of pounds and the wood may not have been anything like as good quality. The boards are over an inch thick and they're solid they don't even flex if you hold them at one end. Billy fitted as few as he could initially because he did not want them to get damaged and at the very least, we knew they would get filthy dirty.

We were advised to cover them in plastic, but I have always been as environmentally friendly as I can be, and I knew not only would the plastic be thrown away it would only be used once, useless for anything else, so I decided not to. We put fabric sheets down that could be washed and/or used again to apply wax, but they just moved, eventually we just left the wood and let it get dirty. We found at the end of the build when we sanded the floor boards it down prior to waxing that we had need not worry, the quality of the wood was so good it came out looking beautiful. Sanding it down was one of the last jobs we did, and it didn't take long. We hired a belt sander and it had an extraction bag attached so the dust was minimal. I used 80 grit then 120 then 240 grit sand paper and that seemed to work perfectly. I waxed it with Antique Oak after I finished, I looked back at the results and I could not be happier, I knew putting such good quality wood on the floor would transform the boat and it did.

The boat sides were lined with tongue and groove wood as was the ceiling, apart from being covered in thick grease all the wood seemed in pretty good condition and again Billy and I had a difference of opinion. I was happy for it to be sanded down and waxed, Billy wanted to remove it and replace it with better quality wood, this is easy to say when you are not paying for it. We both stood our ground and argued our cases until Billy eventually won. Again, the clever lad was right, as there had clearly been a fire at some time that had burnt the rafters in the ceiling and most of the wiring was in poor condition, some had been burnt. It was hard to say what had started the fire, but it was possibly the fire itself or an electrical fault, either way I am so glad it got stripped back, and at this point I was kind of learning just to say yes as my opinion was invariably wrong.

Internal wood cladding

❖ ❖ ❖

But I did have one successful brain wave and that was to extend the back of the boat and make a seating area from where Billy could drive the boat in comfort. As usual Billy's wacky and eccentric little mind went into overdrive and it wasn't long before I was crawling around in my florescent waistcoat in Ken Allan's scrap yard at Morecambe looking for a suitable rear seat out of a car to be made into our sofa.

I wanted a leather sofa at the rear of the boat, but the cheapest good quality small one that I found to be suitable was £600 so again we had to have a re- think. I didn't want to scrimp on quality, but I certainly did want to on price and again, we were supposed to be keeping the build to a budget, so £600 on a sofa was a definite no no. That's when he came up with the car back seat idea and we managed to get a leather one from an Audi A4 and hats off to Audi, it's quality and comfortable. The other thing is it can stand getting wet if you need the doors open for any manoeuvring in poor weather. All Billy had to do was make a frame for it and make it secure he welded a frame and bolted it onto the rear of the boat thus extending it the width of an Audi A4 rear seat. He fitted the seat and later made a cupboard underneath which housed the dining table and he also made concealed cupboards either side of our new sofa.

One of the biggest expenditures was the wood for the canopy frame and the wood for the windscreen frame. Including the frames for the bedrooms it all added up to about £500. We went in Vera and bought all this at once Billy wanted to have everything ready as he was now going to cut where the windscreen was to be. Not only would this leave the boat open to the elements, but it would not be secure, so we had to be ready straight away to build the frame and secure the boat.

Prior to the rear cut the back was just a vertical panel and in the middle was a small narrow doorway which was perfectly fine to use if you were under 4ft 10 and had a figure like Kate Moss.

As Billy had put an extension on the rear of the boat this meant we could move the whole of the kitchen up to where the canvas canopy area used to be, and make it more spacious, it totally transformed the boat. The engine is underneath this part so effectively underneath the kitchen, Billy had to ensure that he could still ac-

Jayne Walden

cess the engine without any disruption to the kitchen units etc. He made a hatch that opened in the floor, you can just push it and it comes up on two hydraulic rams, so unless you know it's there you cannot see it and there is no handle to stand on or trip over. Also, around the engine there is a lot of wasted space, Billy was able to make under floor storage which was invaluable, especially for your dirty items e.g. tools, coal etc, he still managed to leave enough room to maintain the engine and for it to run effectively.

Most of our outlay in money was on the wood, it was becoming a financial nightmare and apart from using it for the frames for the rooms etc, neither of us were happy with the quality to use it for the wood that was going to be on show. We went to one of the suppliers and it was bent even before we were going to purchase it, so we had to have a re think. I sourced a company that dealt in reclaimed wood and we went to have a look, we managed to purchase some superb boarding. Some of it was old scaffold board but we also managed to get a large crate of oak parquet and we got all this for an absolute bargain price of £100. The wood reclaimed from older properties was a thousand times better quality than the new we were buying, I believe we saved over £2000 by doing this, possibly more with the oak parquet, something we would never have dreamed of even looking at in our budget.

When we got home, we just carried it all out of Vera plonked it all in a pile and belt sanded it in one swoop, piece after piece until it was all done, and it looked beautiful, the grain was gorgeous, and we had not even waxed it yet. Billy built the kitchen units out of the board and made the work surfaces out of the oak parquet. Then one day when we were on our travels we were driving past a Christian centre and there was a man putting an old pot sink into a skip, we stopped, and he gladly gave it to us and that's the story of where the sink came from!

One of the things that really put me off buying a narrow boat apart from the price was the stairs, they are so darn narrow. You must make a death defying leap every time you want to go into the boat, they are too narrow and too steep, you need to have tiny little feet just for them to fit on the step. As you are negotiating the doll house sized stairs you also must achieve this bent over double to avoid hitting your head on the roof as you go down. There is only one way to do it; sideways, so your feet can fit on the narrow steps, then grab anything that's available to steady yourself and then launch yourself downstairs as if you're on the parallel bars.

Now, I'm only 5ft 5 but I had to duck going down and coming up was no different. On return I then had to haul myself up, whilst I ducked. Even with my size fives I had to shimmy up and down side ways, I detested the steps, all narrowboat steps should go into room 101, no argument. I was convinced that I was going to break my ankle on every descent, so I said to Billy not only could they not be steep, they had to be wide enough, so I could walk down in high heels, not holding anything without fear of death or at least serious injury.

I wanted to be like in one of those old films where the stunning lady floats down the spiral staircase in her flowing gown with arms elegantly falling by her sides and she looks seductively at the handsome man as she comes down and never has to worry about a step. Yeah yeah, I know that's slightly excessive and there was no handsome man, but you get the point I'm getting at.

Billy pulled it off yet again and the steps are mega, they are just exactly what I wanted, and you can go up and down without holding onto anything even George didn't need to duck. Billy cut both metal sides out and widened the area for the steps. He made each step out of scaffolding board which not only gave it a large surface area to foot fall on, but they can also take the weight of people endlessly stomping up and down on them. He also made each step with a lift top and this space is the most useful in the boat, you can just put anything in and it's so easily accessible.

Not content with all that I also had another request, there was little point cutting a large proportion of the boat roof off to make it open then the minute you walked down the stairs you were presented with a solid wall, yet I wanted two separate bedrooms and

Jayne Walden

a bathroom, I don't demand a lot in a 45ft boat do I?

Have you seen the word bathroom? Yes, it had to have a bath, not unusual in a larger narrowboat, but I wanted a bathroom with everything else, in a 45ft boat! We got a bath for free that had come out of a static caravan and that fitted in perfectly, I tiled round the edges I managed to get some handmade Italian tiles from the charity shop. Most of the extras were sourced from charity shops or reclamation yards, for example, the cattle yokes for the curtain rails, the wallpaper, the oak panelling in the bathroom and the coat hooks. As much as we could we used reclaimed, vintage or antique materials.

Billy gave the illusion that the boat appeared larger and more open, your eyes did not stop until they hit a solid wall. When you looked down the stairs into the main body of the boat, he built a curved wall out of glass blocks, the effect was outstanding and to add to the look they even light up at night. I don't think anyone could have imagined just how good they were going to look.

George was extremely impressed especially with the light they allowed in, he thought that it was an excellent idea. I was over the moon with the result. I wanted to do the whole bathroom out of glass and mirrors to make it look fresh and bigger. The glass blocks were hard to source at the right price, there seemed to be loads in London but none within a reasonable travelling distance, some people wanted £10 a block and this would of just been too expensive, eventually we got some for £1.80 a block but there were two different styles, we just used one style for the dividing wall between Billy's room and the bathroom and one style for the wall as soon as you walked into the boat.

Billy had never fitted glass blocks before, I looked online and it said you needed a fitting kit. I rang a lot of stores and no one had one, but when I investigated it the fitting kit consisted of thin metal rods, tape, tile adhesive, spacers and foam, so I just bought them separately minus the tape and the spacers. The reason for not buying the tape was I couldn't see why I needed it on top of the tile adhesive, metal rods and glue foam. I was building a small bathroom wall not the Forth Road Bridge and the reason for not buying the spacers was I couldn't find any and the expense. This may sound a bit tight fisted and you may think just how expensive some plastic spacers can be, I don't know, but even if they're £10, it's a tenner saved and believe me when you're doing a build as big as this unless you're loaded every tenner adds up and lots of tenner's make a huge saving.

Glass blocks in the curved wall

❖ ❖ ❖

Billy used off cuts of wood instead and just cut them all down to the same size to space them. I don't know if what he did was correct but all I can say is the wall doesn't move and impressed George Clarke so that will do me. Billy put a piece of 3" x 2" screwed to the floor this gave a frame to adhere too but also a line for him to follow, without the wood as a guide it would have been easy to go off course. Billy then put the first course straight onto that and put that on with tile adhesive, he put a metal rod vertical in between each block and then he put in metal wall ties that you would just use on ordinary bricks in between each tile. He left this course to dry and then in between each tile he put expanding foam. It was my job to grout between the blocks and it was so laborious, it does not help that I have the attention span of a newt.

The grouting though was a little more difficult than usual as I said previously the job was to be done on a budget and we ended up 6 blocks short and had to make do with some smaller ones. The funny thing was they looked great against the bigger blocks, but I had to use an enormous amount of grout as the gaps were so wide. It took a day to grout and for the next 3 nights I had pins and needles all down my right arm when I woke up the next morning as I had mixed so much grout.

The boat had a little multi fuel stove on it when we bought it, we used it in the first winter prior to starting the renovation of the boat and it was incredible how efficient it was. It was Billy's idea to put a Rayburn in and I thought he was absolutely barking. I could not believe that you could put the weight of a Rayburn on a boat. The fact that the boats had originally been made for carrying about 30 tonnes of cargo never entered my head and I never gave it a second thought that the boat men wouldn't bother weighing and ballasting everything. They were hardly going to place every piece of coal precisely in each side of the boat to ballast it. So again, my worries were unfounded, but I did manage to keep my worries well and truly in the forefront of my mind until the day the Rayburn was in situ.

I have no experience with Rayburn's, but I know a little about Aga's. My mum had an Aga that was fitted by an 'expert' and he disconnected the back boiler and said it would be fine to run it like that, and it was for a few years. Then one evening when I had left my mums to go home, I had thankfully, forgotten something in her kitchen, my mother was in bed in the bedroom directly above the Aga. When I walked into the kitchen the kitchen unit next to the Aga, was on fire. Over the years the Aga had burnt a hole in the boiler, I later found out that the boiler is designed to constantly have water in it and as the water goes round the radiators it comes back cooling the boiler so it never gets to a tremendous heat a thermostat allows it to be released before it can do that.

Now this proves that even experts can make mistakes, so we didn't feel worried about doing it ourselves. I did ask around for advice and 90% of people incredibly said if you leave the back boiler with the pipes free and not constricted it will be fine. If you block the pipes any water left in will steam and it will go off like a bomb. I was not happy with leaving the back boiler in place, so Billy and I researched and took a different approach. Billy cut the top off the boiler and filled it with fire brick so effectively it's not there. We could not use it to run a radiator or warm water as it needs a constant supply of water. So, it was not an easy job to do and you must get the correct advice prior to doing it, my mother's Aga setting on fire was a strange blessing in disguise, because had this not happened, I would have taken the 'experts' advice and left the boiler empty. Billy has sealed it extremely well with fire blocks, board and cement and you cannot feel the heat to the outside walls Billy with his alterations, has changed entirely the fire housing, grate and boiler of the Rayburn to ensure we do not have a similar accident to my mothers.

We have a smoke alarm and carbon monoxide alarm next to it, a twin wall flue is a must, the heat a Rayburn gives off is incredible and you don't want the flue to set fire to your boat. Also, the boat as you know is narrow and if any one tripped and a hand went out and touch the twin wall it would be unpleasant to the touch, but if you fell on a single wall flue you could potentially give yourself very bad burns, I have seen them glow red before. The Rayburn keeps us toasty warm and you can cook a full Sunday dinner on it no problem, its cheap to run and when closed it will stay alight all night.

I had to source the Rayburn which was a feat. I trawled the internet again and they were either completely knackered or down south, where everything I want to buy seems to be, nobody seems to sell anything apart from baby clothes or mobile phones within a 100-mile radius of my house. We eventually managed to get one from the other side of Bradford, I needed a few counselling sessions to just think about going to pick it up, that ring road around Bradford is a living hell. A constant stream of unnecessary traffic lights that stop you even when you are the only car in the vicin-

Jayne Walden

ity, believe me I went through at 2.00 am and slept in Vera's cab at the other end just to avoid driving through Bradford in the day time.

The Rayburn was only £180 so you are getting a lot for your money especially if you use it in a house and it heats the water and all the rooms. The reason they are so cheap second hand is because they are a nightmare to move, they are unbelievably heavy. The people we bought ours from had a fork lift truck and they lifted it on to our trailer from smooth tarmac. We, however, at the other end did not have a fork lift truck and we were based in a field.

Now as I said a lovely couple from Galgate had allowed us to moor next to their land, but they worked away and one of the stipulations was the gate to the field was kept locked; which was fine as lifting wood etc over a gate was much easier than carrying it all the way down the canal towpath, also no members of the public could moan at us if we left anything outside the boat whilst we refurbished her. So, initially the 5-bar gate was of no concern to us until that is my son buys an approximately 400 kg Rayburn and wants to lift it over it.

I am eccentric and I'm not a sheep, so I do not follow the conformists with their new car and their 2.4 children families. I do as I please regardless of what critics may say, and I don't care what people think and if it goes wrong, we'll learn from our mistakes and try again and usually have a damn good laugh in the meantime. But I was a little concerned about the proposed Rayburn launch and the big watery thing it may fall into. There is always someone that has their phone at the ready and would rather film you to get some shares, likes and recognition on social media rather than help. I explained this to Billy, who detests social media and I explained some numpty will film the Rayburn as it free falls into the canal, Billy really didn't care and just went ahead regardless.

We arrived home with the Rayburn and Billy did an expert job of stripping it down to the bare minimum, I was amazed how much was in there, he basically stripped it down to a metal rectangle. I took one look at his achievement and honestly thought I could just pick it up myself, but even with everything taken off it was incredible how heavy it was. Words failed me when Billy said we would have to lift it over the 5-bar gate, I just knew we were ending up on YouTube with about 1 million views, but he was adamant, and he was doing it and that was that.

I thought of his strongest friend and telephoned them, they were as willing as Billy, thought we were absolutely barking mad, but they were willing to make total fools of themselves as well. We used two of the floor boards to shunt the Rayburn into the back of Vera and we set off to our destination. I already had clear visions of the crane lifting the Rayburn out of the canal and that was my only worry, not anyone's unwanted opinion, just the thought of hell from the Canal and River Trust as a Rayburn was sticking out of the canal.

I reversed Vera up to the gate until she touched it and we used the same scaffolding boards to get the Rayburn out of Vera, we used straps to keep it upright and basically slid the Rayburn down onto a waiting sturdy trolley and all went remarkably well. We then shoved, pushed and hauled, did anything we could to get it over the bumpy ground to the boat. I was fine hauling a Rayburn down the field to the canal, but now I went into full panic mode at the thought of it going over the canal into the boat. What if it tipped the boat over as it rested on the edge I thought, but Billy just kept nagging at me to hurry up and get on with the job in hand. We used the same boards to make a bridge to go across the banking of the canal to the edge of the boat. The problem with this was it was during a long dry spell of weather and the canal water was low, so you couldn't get the boat near the banking, so we were having to push the Rayburn quite a distance on the boards across the canal.

It felt like eternity as we pushed and pulled the Rayburn across the canal to the boat. We finally got it to the boat and rested it on the edge as we now had to lift it down into the boat. I could not believe it when the Rayburn was sitting on the edge of the boat the boat didn't even notice, she never moved an inch, the weight was irrelevant to her and we just slid the Rayburn on and in it went. It was such a massive relief.

Initially we were going to fit it in front of the stairs, parallel to them and leave a passage way down the side, but because Billy had made so much more room in the rear extension this would not have worked as well as putting it at the side of the boat which is what we ended up doing. Another reason for wanting it across the boat was weight distribution, but the bathroom is opposite the Rayburn and there is quite a lot of weight in all those blocks, not as much as a Rayburn though so we had to add some gravel (to the ballast) to counteract the weight of the Rayburn, but it didn't take much to balance it out correctly.

Once the Rayburn was fitted it made the boat cosy and was very useful, I rarely use the gas to heat water, a pan warms up in minutes and I use that for washing pots etc. I have a clothes drier above and the heat it gives off there is never any damp about, I could not recommend a Rayburn more.

The Rayburn (positioned but not fitted)

❖ ❖ ❖

As I have spoken about previously the main thing I wanted was for the boat to look open, and managing this feat when it is only 6ft wide and you want to fit two bedrooms and a bathroom on is not an easy task. Billy pulled this off perfectly as you look down from the back of the boat the glass wall is a stunning feature and it commands you to look at it. Having a certain amount of transparency allows your eye to look on and effectively look through it. Curving the glass wall was genius, not only did it add that extra few inches of space, which was not lost in the bathroom, Billy just shaped the edge of the bath to fit so no actual space in the bath was lost. The curve opened the hallway, your eye looks round it and gives the illusion of being wider than it is.

It makes the hallway look shorter, because also at the other end of the passageway at Matilda's bedroom end, he curved the wall there also. He then put a double strip of glass blocks on Matilda's curved end wall, again giving more light but also the illusion of space. As well as a bath, Billy managed to fit a full kitchen, seated dining area, large log store, Rayburn, two private bedrooms and a sitting room all in a 45ft boat and believe me it's not cramped. Also, because Billy curved the bathroom wall it made quite a good-sized passage way, so much so that I managed to fit a desk next to the Rayburn and this is where I wrote this book from, so effectively he fit a small office in there too.

It didn't matter how we measured the layout of the new build we could not fit a bathroom in correctly and two decent sized bedrooms with the window lay out as it was, so one window had to go. Billy blocked off the first window opposite the Rayburn, he did the work to such a high standard you cannot tell a window has ever been there. He plated and welded the space that was left when he had removed the window and it was much better once it was gone. There was no loss of light as we had opened the front up and as the old window was just below the front screen the front screen replaced any light lost by the removal of the old window and light flooded in.

What we had not also realised was that it was so much more private when Billy blocked it off. This also allowed him to make a bench seat opposite the Rayburn as behind the seat was now a wall and you can now sit back in privacy, storage was also made underneath this. The bench is fab, if your cooking, in between tasks you can just sit back and relax looking up through the large window at the clear blue sky or stars twinkling in the night sky.

Also, when visitors come, they can sit on the bench chatting as you cook, it just works perfectly.

The steps are so large and solid often without thinking people plonk themselves down on them, they are now so wide there is still plenty of room to safely pass someone sitting on the stairs and that's in a narrow boat!

Billy's bedroom was the easiest to do, he just didn't care so long as he had a bed in that's all he was bothered about, so he just has a bed with storage and a table, a far cry from Matilda, who wanted everything crammed into a 6ft space. Billy made Matilda's bed higher than normal and then underneath he put a shelf which housed lots of stacker boxes for storage, it was amazing how much room there was under the bed especially with the shelf being there as well. She can fit all her toys including what must be the world's largest Lego collection and all her clothes under there. Heightening the bed also gave her a good sized area to play in, she's also managed to put her own twist on space saving managing to fit the family dog in there, which is a good sized lurcher and she has fit Dougal our pygmy hedgehog as well, the funny thing is they don't seem cramped as they endlessly watch her play Barbie. Once let loose in there she plastered pictures of unicorns on every available surface from the curtains to the lights.

I was the least worried about my bedroom, my theory is I have had my childhood and they can never get theirs back so unselfishly make it the best you can for them with what you have got. So, Matilda having her own bedroom and play area was the most important thing in my eyes. My bedroom doubles up as the seated area at the front. Billy made it so that the sofa pulled out into a double bed and lying in bed in the morning looking out over the canal through the bi fold doors, or, in the summer allowing the warm breeze to flow over you is a good enough substitute for any private bedroom for me. The bi-fold doors were a superb idea of Billy's the light they let in and the openness of the outside they give you is awesome. Throughout the whole of the boat Billy managed to incorporate storage, down the passage way he even had hidden cupboards and the step at the front is a storage area, even with the three of us and two animals there is plenty of room and storage.

I had never heard of LED lighting prior to the build and now I just cannot recommend it enough, it uses a tiny amount of electric and it is so bright. I bought LED strip lights and Billy ran them down the side of the sliding roof. They are just a flexible strip with a sticky back and you just peel of the backing and stick them where ever you want. I also had an idea to put them along each course of glass blocks, so at night you can switch them on and they shine through the tiles the effect is amazing. I thought this was my unique idea, until I saw some for sale with them already incorporated, I was still happy in the knowledge though that my strip lights cost £19.99 whereas it was hundreds of pounds to purchase glass blocks that had lights already fitted and the effect from mine was just the same. We only needed 6 lights for the rest of the boat as the LED ones are so bright, if there had not been any walls in the boat and it was just open plan two would have been enough, but we needed one in each room and one for the bathroom. The lights were so cheap, and they have never gone dim however much we use them, they just attach to a 12-volt battery which can either be charged by the running of the boat or solar or both, ours is attached to both.

So that is basically most of the build covered without going into the nitty gritty and obvious things like that we painted the outside etc, the only other thing left is to talk about the stress which I am not going to lie to you it was immense.

We found out our reveal date quite late on in the build, it was to be the 14th October we were told this date was a definite on the 30th September, by this date we only had 14 days left to finish the build and I was panicking. The main cuts front and back were completed and the outside was 90% complete and inside the frames of the bedroom walls were up and the ceiling of the whole boat was ply lined, papered and painted, but no matter how hard we tried and how much work we did and however many hours we put in progress seemed to be slow.

The weather had now turned against us and it seemed impossible to get the back of the boat painted. There wasn't any howling gales nor heavy downfall, but you would just get the boat dry and it was if God just emptied a watering can full of water out just enough to dampen the surface again. We later realised we were making sterling progress and there is a point where everything just comes together, but for us at the time it felt like we were working at a snail's pace.

Unfortunately, we only really realised we were going to pull it off about 12 hours prior to a very famous, distinguished gentleman not only with his own TV programmes but with his own production company coming to have a look at what we had achieved! What we had not realised was the sheer scale of the project we had taken on, me, because I'm a complete amateur and a bit dim and Billy because of his youth. With us both having a care free attitude to life and that lack of experience and we had got ourselves into another fine mess. We now knew we had taken on a massive project and we had done well to pull it off. It was not until George came to see us and we could see how visibly shocked he was about how much we had taken on and achieved in our time scale, it was only then we realised just how much we had achieved.

The first day of filming was in July and we were filmed stripping the inside of the boat out. When we started work it gave us about 10 weeks to complete the build. When you are being filmed there is a lot of repetition and so on film days progress was slow.

For example, one day was taken up filming us cooking tea as a family so no work on the boat was done that whole day. On another day our faithful generator that had never failed us in 5 years decided to have a strop, the thing was it only decided to have a strop after Billy and I had carried it 1/4 mile down the canal towpath and it is not light. After about an hour of tinkering it was clear she was not playing ball, I had to then set off to a friend's house to pick up his generator, by the time I had returned half a day had gone. Had the film crew not been there we would have got on with a job that did not need electricity and mended the generator later which is what Billy did. But the crew were there, and they needed to film the work that needed electricity as the next day they had filming work elsewhere, so this is something that you need to allow for if you were to apply to go on a similar programme and to allow for in the timescale of your build.

On the first day we were filmed we started off bounding about like two energetic puppies' excited about going out for walkies, it was all great fun and we were going to be on the telly, so it was all very jolly. We really had not bargained for what we had let ourselves in for. We now know we did not take the first few weeks seriously enough, ten weeks felt like eternity, we even went away rallying for one of the weekends.

On the days we did work we did not put the hours in and they were too short, we also never stayed over in Vera. Had we of done so we could have just got out of bed and got straight into work. By the end of August reality had hit me hard, but Billy is still only very young, and you know what it's like when your young, time goes so slowly, and you never think anything is going to come around, but it does, and the 14th of October was stomping home at a remarkable rate.

Billy was still bounding around in his puppy stage, but I'd grown up into the wise old matriarch remarkably quickly, and Billy needed a very big push to get motivated. Thankfully, it sunk in and by the beginning of September we were at full steam ahead and apart from a few commitments we had to attend, this gave us about 6 weeks to steam ahead and complete.

It was extremely tough but it's all a learning curve and on the next build time management will be a priority. Leaving it late put us under immense pressure. I believe adding the time up we did the build in about 6-8 weeks. If you are going to take on a build that is to be filmed remember you also must work round the film crew. So, when your told you have 10 weeks, even if you want to work every day you may not be able to, as you may have to wait if it's something they want to film.

They are constantly booked going from one location to another, so you may have a glorious day where you want to paint and until you put the paint on you cannot get on with the next job ie sign writing, but the film crew want to film you painting but they cannot come to film it for 3 days, this puts you back and we had not allowed for this in the build.

Remember the production company have invested thousands in the making of the programme, so they need to make it a success. If you cannot be flexible, personally, I wouldn't apply, because everybody needs to work around everyone else, if you let the crew down it's like a domino effect and that topples everyone, they then need to rearrange everything to put you into a filming slot again. Remember they are taking the risks they have built the programme up prior to you even being about and yes, they need you to make the programme but there are plenty of others. Just the one programme and it's you that wants a piece of it, so you need to live it if you're going to be successful. We did live it apart from practicalities we worked round the crew being available whenever they asked the only time, we put them off was when it could not be help i.e., they wanted to film the windows being put in and the glass had not arrived. When we were constantly doing the build living it day in day out, we did not realise how much progress we were making, add to that the tiredness, lack of sleep, constantly feeling dirty you can understand why it gets a bit stressful.

One thing it did do was make me appreciate things more. I remember going to bed one evening and it was just one of the many nights where I hadn't slept the previous evening. When I got into bed, I knew I was only going to get two hours sleep at the most. I lay there feeling physically and mentally exhausted, I felt sick and I wanted to cry. I had a makeshift bed for another night. I could feel the sanded paint in my hair and all around my body. I had worked alone the night before as Billy had to sleep, as he was working power tools, being the ultimate gentleman he did not want to go to bed and leave me to work, he hated leaving me to work alone, but I forced him to get some sleep, it was just not worth the risk.

I could carry on even as tired as I was, I could not do a lot of damage to myself with a paintbrush. As I lay in bed exhausted, I thought of the soldiers in the wars and although I have always had the utmost respect for them, doing the build really drove home what sheer hell they went through. Here I was crying and whining because I felt a bit hard done to because I had not had any sleep or a proper wash or meal for a few days, the difference was I had chosen to do this. What, I had not thought of was I had things soldiers would have given their right arm for; warmth, security, a dry bed, rest when I really needed it and I never feared for my life! Even though my bed was not comfy, it was a bed and it was dry, even though the food was basic it was there when I needed it and I never went hungry and had I wanted too I could have gone home to a comfy bed, a hot shower and eaten what I wanted, so I re-evaluated my situation and realised in the grand scheme of things, things were not that bad. I was in a fortunate position and George and the producers had trusted in Billy, even though Billy was still a child, they took a big risk trusting him to pull this off. So, in the morning I stopped moaning, thanked my lucky stars, got my big butt out of bed and got my head down, made sure that my cup was half full not half empty, and knew that I was going to complete this build what ever happened.

Things changed from that day, just ask the poor dog walker who passed chuckling to himself as I belted out 'Don't Stop Me Now', I think even Freddie Mercury would have been proud. I had not seen or heard the walker coming and I was in the rear of the boat with all the windows surrounding me and the curtains were not up yet, I could not have been more exposed if I was on stage.

I had fallen in the canal a couple of times throughout the build and I really don't know how and neither did Billy. One minute I was painting the boat and the next minute 'plop' I was in the water to my waist, when this happened my reaction was totally over the top especially the second time when I curled up on the banking in the foetal position crying. I had though badly twisted my knee this time, so I had a bit of an excuse. But after evaluating everything I then again plopped into the canal for no reason and Billy who was inside the boat at the time heard, "Oh no, not again". But rather than make a big song and dance about it I hauled myself out onto the embankment and sloped off back to Vera to change, once in dry clothes, I just got back on with the job, I had learnt to deal with my emotions far better at this point.

The next morning after my 2 hours sleep, I was up at 6.30 am and finished at 2.30 am and apart from 20 mins for lunch and a half hour phone call to a mate I never stopped, but there still seemed like there was loads to do. We knew from now on there was no going home, and we now knew we were living in the boat, we even sent Matilda and the dog packing to her Grandmas for the final few days. She was a very upset little girl not being able to see her mummy, but she fully understood it was a necessity. Deep down she knew she was better being at Grandmas being waited on hand and foot and having Barbie and Lego on tap rather than been shunted around the boat at 30-minute intervals as we needed to refurbish the place she was situated at.

After she got snuggled in at Grannies, she never asked to come back anyway, so we knew it was for the best. If we were realistically going to finish in time, we needed to increase the pace and make the situation easier for ourselves, because we couldn't put any more hours in.

I believe that if we had added up the days that we worked on the boat, the build took us approximately 6 weeks to complete. Billy was absolutely amazing he just got his head down and worked and worked, he really did the full build himself, yes, I was there grouting tiles and filling and waxing wood, but that's because I

Jayne Walden

wanted to, realistically Billy didn't need me. I couldn't have done what he did, it was awesome to watch all the build coming together and I was so proud of him. How a child could do what he did I don't know, and I know I'll get burnt at the stake by all the feminists but, there was no man there either to help him, Billy was brought up by a single female parent and here he was doing man's things, ahh I'm going to be shot! Not only was he doing man things he was doing it better than many men 2 or 3 times his age.

◆ ◆ ◆

CHAPTER 6

THE FRONT CUT

◆ ◆ ◆

It's now the 26th of September and we are 19 days from our reveal date. The manic panicking has subsided a bit as we feel we are well on our way now. The sheer horror of cutting the front out does not seem as bad now that we have got the back fully secure and water tight. The cameraman has been pushing for Billy to get the front cut done, which is understandable as this gets it out of the way for him and can start to be edited. We, however, have not been so quick to do it, it would have overwhelmed us, there was too much mess and too many places letting the wind and the rain in, we would have felt like we were going backwards. However, now that we are further on and the back is water tight and the ceilings wall papered and the bath in etc, we feel happy to go ahead. The filming crew arrived at 9 am in the morning at my mother's home to film Billy making the bi-folding doors which need to be ready to fit immediately, again due to weather and security. Bi-fold doors are a series of doors which fold onto each other, these are not easy to make even for a carpenter with years of experience so for a teenager it's amazing. Billy made them himself, which was later to be confirmed by somebody as experienced and talented as George Clarke when we heard his surprise when Billy said he made them himself. George asked him numerous times just to double check as he was amazed that a teenager had made them. He kept on so much Billy was pressured into giving another answer, so when George said, "So you made them all yourself," Billy said, "Yeah apart from the brass hinges," To which George replied; " Well it would not have surprised me if you made them too!"

Billy had to have the skill and determination to make them perfectly because if he did not get them right or even if they were slightly out, they would not have opened or closed properly. Also, the draught would make the boat cold and uncomfortable and obviously the damp and rain would get in. As I said previously George was flabbergasted to say the least that Billy had made them himself, but not only had Billy achieved this he had had to make the doors under the pressure of being filmed and a camera being inches away from him and recording his every move and relentless questions from the crew. The cameramen did not miss a trick and short of filming Billy going for a pee they wanted to film his every move, even when we believed it was boring and often repetitive. Looking back, they would also need to cover themselves, they were putting their neck on the line risking filming with a kid, especially with a short crucial time frame and such a massive project, it wasn't like Billy was making a den out of a horse trailer he was completely re-building and designing a narrowboat and he was a so young!

Understandably most people would be a little sceptical that a child could manage this near impossible feat single handed, so I believe (this was never said to me) that to cover themselves they basically filmed the whole build. George had his superb reputation to lose, remember they had never met us, did not know us, we could be a couple of deranged fantasists that had never even picked up a chisel, never mind have the ability to refurbish a boat or Billy might (which some people may of thought) had a nice dad that was secretly doing the work for him and allowing Billy to take all the credit, but this could not be further from the truth.

But you know what it's like now, some people will do anything for a few shares on social media, but neither were true, Billy is extremely talented, and he did every bit of the build himself, apart from the curtains! The camera crew had captured every move of his to prove this.

The cutting out was very hard, I don't know how the hell Billy managed to even lift the cutter they are that heavy never mind put enough pressure on to cut and protect himself from it slipping and cutting himself in half. The cutting seemed to go on forever the constant noise and sparks flying, but eventually he was through the sheet of metal cutting away the sheet with its small holes in, where there was once a small window and an Alice in Wonderland door.

Billy and Matilda taking a break

❖ ❖ ❖

The front panel of the boat was hanging on for dear life by a metal slither, then whack, one swing with the sledge hammer and the front panel of the boat was gone and a big gaping hole took its place, but there was no fear, no regrets, it looked awesome and I knew we had done the right thing and I could not wait for the doors to be fitted.

Cameras finished filming they had their excitement, they didn't wait around to see it get put back together, they always wanted to leave this bit till the reveal. After filming it was late and we realised we had less than 18 days to go to the reveal and the front part of the boat was missing, yikes!

We worked until 12 that night and Billy got the door frames in which looked great. I was up at 5am the next morning and got the other side of the boat painted. Finally, I could get the rest of the boat apart from the back painted, Producers had asked me hold off this painting until after the last time they filmed before the reveal date. It was such a concern as it was a big area to paint and progress was dependent on the weather which we were not having much luck with.

So, when I got up the next morning it was dry, there was no coffee for me, just straight out to the boat to get the first coat on, the change was instant with every swipe of the brush the deep colour covered over the old tired ghastly green and with every stroke the old girl transformed some more, wiping away the ugly duckling to allow the beautiful swan to shine through. After every few strokes I would step back and admire her, it brought a tear to my eye. I know initially she looked like a bit of a joke boat, nobody would have looked twice, but now she was growing up and looking like a proper boat, like she meant business she only needed a bit of TLC to bring the real beauty out in her.

I was amazed how quickly I got the first coat on. I had let Billy have a lie in and set his alarm for 7am after I had put the first coat on, I made a coffee and sat on our sofa waiting for the paint to dry. Now this is how tired we had become, Billy had gone to bed walking past 45ft of green painted boat, when he woke only a handful of hours later he walked past 45ft of gleaming bright red boat, he walked into the rear of the boat and I was beaming from ear to ear relishing in the glory of my achievement and the awesome transformation of the boat.

Billy walked in said the usual morning pleasantries and put the kettle on not a word, nada, zilch, not a murmur. I thought 'how rude' so I asked him had he noticed anything different about the boat and either he was telling the truth, or he should have won an Oscar. So, I told him to go outside and look at the boat, it was nice because I then got to see his initial reaction what a look of surprise.

Billy then had his coffee and went off to fit the doors, which he did with remarkable ease and wow did they look good, they looked amazing. Prior to the front being cut out, if anything happened outside ie Matilda shouted for me to take a look at something, or I heard a noise I had to physically get up and peer out of the window, then maybe a couple of others dependent on where the thing was you wanted to view, if you didn't get the window right first time the thing you wanted to view had usually gone. Now you could just move your head and see around most of the boat it was fantastic and I loved it, there was nearly a full panoramic view from the front it was awesome and so satisfying, once again a mad panic and worry and putting something off and it had again paid off, Billy was right once again!

Bi-fold doors (External view)

❖ ❖ ❖

Bi-fold doors (Internal view)

❖ ❖ ❖

I had constantly wondered how we would paint the back of the boat, we did not have a mooring at a marina and this would have been the easiest way. I thought the best way would be to get a small boat, I was surprised how expensive they were, but I put an advert out on social media and thankfully someone wanted rid of one and incredibly it was only at the next bridge down from where we had moored our boat. Matilda and I walked down to get it. We never gave it a second thought of how unstable it would be, we launched it and tied it to the embankment thankfully (said in a sarcastic tone) Billy managed to film the sheer terror rather than help, bit like one of those numpties with their phones, the only difference being it was Matilda any my own choice to put it on YouTube not some strangers.

Anyway, as you will see if you view the video on YouTube, we were not very good at it and if you listen carefully in the video as we're rocking backwards and forwards and I'm screaming in sheer terror Matilda states that we should row up to the Marina and that is about half a mile away!

❖ ❖ ❖

Matilda and Jayne messing about on the river

you tube link
https://youtu.beG9euoSi6Tp8
Youtube user name = matildariver1

❖ ❖ ❖

After filming the front cut Matilda had nagged a guy from the film crew all day to go out in the rowing boat with her and he finally succumbed. He had been very unwilling to go in, but Matilda pulled the boat up to the side of the banking and in he got. Then the only problem was getting him out, he was rowing up and down the canal even when the other camera man was calling him to leave for home, he loved it. We all then messed about in the boat filming them for a change, it was nice just to have a mess about for a while and momentarily forget about the enormous task that still lay ahead for us with very few days left until the final reveal.

Jayne Walden

Matilda and a cameraman messing about on the canal

◆ ◆ ◆

CHAPTER 7

THE REVEAL

◆ ◆ ◆

The Reveal day had finally arrived, and we were all beyond excited, Matilda was hyper, and she was manically asking the crew repetitive questions as she could not contain how excited she was, she particularly targeted the director. The director was lovely and coped extremely well with the assault of questions fired at her from Matilda, which was to go on throughout the day. She wanted to know everything about her from her marital status to what she had for tea the night before.

We all stood at the gate waiting patiently for the main man to arrive. I looked up at the sky and apart from one solitary aeroplane trail it was clear blue without a cloud. I prayed for it to stay that way and that we would have a dry reveal. Then a wave of excitement rippled through the group here he was, Billy looked like the cat that got the cream, a white van pulled up and out jumped George. The funny thing was I then automatically stepped back like Prince Philip would allowing his Queen to go forward.

This was Billy's day George Clarke would not be coming to our home without Billy's skills, so I gave him the respect he had earnt and let him have the glory of meeting George first. Thank fully Matilda was so besotted with Georges Director she took little interest in George and let Billy bathe in the glory. George looked exhausted, later in the day, when he explained his work schedule we knew why. George then launched his hand out to shake Billy's hand and then mine, the day we had worked endlessly through blood (I cut myself quite a lot!) tears and sweat had arrived.

Then a moment came which we were just not prepared for, George turned to the director and said "no one told me that this had been upgraded to the main build," having never met George and just the way he said it both Billy and I really thought he was joking until the director said " Yes we thought we would leave it until the last minute to tell you"' I wish I could of got a picture of the look on Billy's face he beamed from ear to ear, I threw my arms round him and congratulated him on his massive achievement, tears rolling down my face. We had been told that we were a B build but because of Billy's massive achievement he had been upgraded to an A.

George then explained what we would be doing, and the crew went away to film his introduction. I went up to the house and my mother was nonchalantly reading the newspaper, it was clear she wasn't taking a lot in, I explained that George was here she didn't even look up from her paper, " are you not going to meet him?" I asked, she didn't need any persuasion, she leapt up out of her seat, Usain Bolt had done slower starting times, she was like a Greyhound out of a trap, " Oh can I?" she was already half way out of the door.

We waited for George to finish and then it was our turn to show him Veronica our beloved Volkswagen LT Campervan, the one Billy had refurbished at 15 years old. Billy beamed from ear to ear with pride as George walked over to Veronica and George and the cameraman prepared to go in and see her for the first time. Obviously, George needs to know the plan of the day and an idea what he is doing and as he heads the programme I'm sure his opinion of who goes on the programme is very relevant, but apart from the basics, George does not get to see what he is entering so that they can catch his expression and his reaction is natural. I was asked not to go in Veronica when they revealed her to George, boo hoo, I would have loved to see the reaction on George's face. I heard him though and wow, unbelievable and a lot of other words to express George's surprise were heard.

George was aghast when he walked into Veronica, you could hear it in his voice, he wasn't just doing it to make good telly he was genuinely in shock, he could not believe the work had been carried out by a then 15-year-old, all by himself. Billy had done the work all himself, with no help from anyone, he wanted to do it this way, a determined stubborn little s**t at 15 and I'm glad he refused help because it made it his baby, no one can ever take away from him that he completed a camper van before his 16th birthday by himself.

Transforming it from a dilapidated old horsebox, full of mouldy hay, manure and rotten urine-soaked boards, he had even managed to remove the ancient heavy ramp with those stubborn strong steel springs by himself, how? I don't know, beggar's belief but he did. I had made the curtains and that was it, George kept referring to this in a light-hearted way and making a joke of it, the comparison of the amount of work I did and the level of skill to Billy's was a little unbalanced to say the least.

George and Billy had gone into the camper van, the producers tell George very little, so they can capture his genuine surprise and they had no problem with this when George entered the van and saw the amazing work Billy had done. You could tell by George's constant vocabulary of; unbelievable, amazing, awesome that he just could not take it all in, he said that an adult with years of experience would be proud of this never mind a child. I knew that we were on a winner now, as much as I adored Veronica and the work Billy had done on it was outstanding and as you will see George will back me up on that, it was nowhere near as mean a feat as the boat. If an architect of Georges calibre was impressed with the camper van, wait until you see the boat I thought, I knew we were onto a winner.

One of the crew had rung earlier in the week to ask if it was okay if the crew and George ate their dinner in my mum's kitchen, obviously I said this was fine, I told my mum who was beside herself with excitement that her favourite presenter was going to be dining in her kitchen. She had already made him a coffee, which had to be perfect just the way George liked it, by George's own admission he was fussy when it came to his coffee, we would never get away with so many demands for the perfect coffee but as I rattled off to my mother how it had to be, she took it in her stride and cradled the cup like a baby as she tottered down the gravel path and presented it to George like he had just been awarded an OBE! It was just short of the curtsy!

The kitchen experience never happened, as Billy had been elevated from a B build to an A build that morning, they needed further footage and pictures, so we shot off to the boat to get what they needed.

A disappointed mother had to just put up with Billy and I for lunch as we were told by production to meet at 1 O'clock. We arrived at the boat and George was filming the introduction further down the canal so was yet to see the boat. We waited for him to finish and then he came up and the camera team prepared everything for him to enter MatildaJayne.

We were still exhausted from the build which we had only manage to complete 12-15 hours prior to George viewing it, so we were still in a bit of a dream world through sheer exhaustion. We were on tender hooks waiting to hear what George had to say about the boat and his opinion on the quality of Billy's work and the design, we stood patiently waiting for him to finish filming.

Jayne Walden

George in the back ground on his phone!

◆ ◆ ◆

It was amazing how many people walked past and took no notice, towards the end when we could relax more George was sitting next to the tow path and people just walked past not even recognising him, but I suppose the last thing you expect to see is George Clarke sitting next to the towpath on the Lancaster Canal.

We were all then given our instructions, which was to wait at the boat whilst George walked up and greeted us, he talked us through what would happen and told me he would give me a kiss, then walk into the boat with Billy. I started taking the micky saying how excited I was. Being a victim of domestic violence, I never got back into a relationship after leaving my abuser so having a kiss from George Clarke even if it was only a friendly peck to greet us was damn exciting for someone who last had male contact in a former life! I started pretending I was all overcome with emotion, but then when filming started, I got what I was supposed to do wrong about 3 times and they had to keep doing more takes, so it back fired on me I really did look like a sad divvy that had got excited over a George Clarke kiss! Anyway, it was very pleasant, and I wasn't going to turn him away!

I wasn't allowed into the boat with George and Billy which I would have loved to of done to see the utter surprise on George's face and Billy beaming with pride when George had recognised his talent and sheer determination to complete such a massive project himself at such a young age. I had no worries that George would not be impressed, you would have to be blind not to see that it was outstanding work and just so remarkable that a child had done it, so for me it was a done deal that George was going to be impressed prior to him even seeing it.

Everything went to plan apart from my instructions, George came along and 3 kisses later, (all the woman are now screaming why did you not keep getting it wrong?? There was only so much I could do before I lost complete self-respect), he shook Billy's hand and they both entered MatildaJayne.

Matilda and I were seated outside, Matilda had a forlorn look on her little face as she wanted to be in there enjoying the moment, she now wanted to be the centre of attention, in her little mind she was the most important person and Billy was just an afterthought who should only got a little look in. The fact of the matter was if it was not for Billy's amazing talent we would not be sitting outside listening to George Clarke and Billy Walden having a chat nor hearing Georges' continual wow, that's amazing, it's unbelievable. I was sitting outside beaming with pride, tears rolling down my face, one proud mother as George continued to relentlessly praise my wonder son. My son had risen above been bullied at school and out shone his critics and incompetent professionals and achieved what many would not attempt to achieve in a lifetime, I was one proud mother and I was going to shout it from the rooftops.

George went through the whole boat amazed at Billy's use of storage, the idea of the folding roof, the Rayburn, wood holder and that he had also managed to incorporate a bath. George was equally impressed with how Billy had used the light with his glass wall and the storage ideas for example underneath Matilda's bed.

Jayne Walden

George mirrored what I though regarding how much Billy had managed to fit inside 45ft long, he talked about how not only he had managed to incorporate a bath and a Rayburn but also 2 private, walled off bedrooms and he said how that it was a remarkable achievement! He commented on how he had managed to do all this yet still make it look so spacious. Even with all the crew in there and George who is not small, you did not feel cramped and when you walk into the boat Billy has made it like it feel like it is open plan, your eye wanders and you want to see what is next, it does not feel blocked off.

When you sit at one end of the boat you can see right to the other end and it looks a good distance away not a mere 45ft. George said its genius, the planning, the architecture, the use of light and again he was amazed Billy has started it at such a young age, being only 17 years old. George said he knows people who have studied at University and had years of experience and couldn't come up with the fool proof design that Billy had accomplished. He was extremely impressed that he had also achieved this with limited resources and certainly limited space out on location.

I'd had total faith in Billy from the start of the build, when Billy built the camper van, I just presumed that when we started using it fully and staying out in it for periods of time that we would realise we had made some mistakes with the planning. For example, a light would shine in your eye when you watched the tv, or a window was at the wrong height for you to enjoy the outside on a rainy day, but I soon realised that I was wrong he had even then at the tender age of 15 got it right. I can honestly say the whole build is perfect, I love Veronica and because he sourced all the best materials albeit second hand to keep costs down or made things himself it never wears, the other thing is because he uses so much quality wood it never gets damp. You know the awful thing that modern caravans do, leave them not in use for a while and the damp creeps in, everything smells fusty, you have to keep a little heater on and anything left up against a side gets mouldy, not in Veronica we left her all winter with no heating on' everything was left in there from bedding to cushions and it all stayed dry and damp free.

After George had gone through the whole of the boat, he sat outside with us and asked us questions on various things like what Matilda and I thought of Billy's skills. It was nice to sit around and have a chat, then all good things come to an end and it was time for George to go, he got up and said his goodbyes and that was that we all looked at each other and it felt strange like we had nothing to do.

The rest of the crew stayed to get some final shots and get some drone coverage, we went to the supermarket and did a proper shop for the first time in six weeks. When we came back the crew were just packing up and we all hugged and said our tearful goodbyes, it was strange leaving people we had spent so much time with and gone through so much with, but that is what the filming industry is like you have to take the work when it comes and everybody was going to their next project all in different places.

We weren't we were going home as a family to a nice hot bath, a decent meal and just to lay back and watch the tv, something we had not done for nearly two months. After tea and a bath, I laid on the sofa half-heartedly watching the television. I could not really concentrate, the thoughts of the day playing through my mind. Eventually though we all drifted off to bed and I must have just zonked out. In the morning I was woken by the daylight, something which had not happened for two months, I had always got up in the dark to work on the boat. I jumped up , shot out of bed screaming "Billy, come on we've slept in," Then the penny dropped, we had no need to panic the build was done , I could stay in bed and relax, or so I thought until Billy said later "You know what we could do?"………………………….

❖ ❖ ❖

The End

Jayne Walden

Thank you for reading and I hope you enjoyed it.

◆ ◆ ◆

Printed in Germany
by Amazon Distribution
GmbH, Leipzig